Prof.Sir.Bashiru Aremu
Prof.Dr.K .Mahammad Rafi
Dr.Mir.Iqbal Faheem
Prof. Mohammed Abdul Nayeem

Doctorate Publications

Imprint

any brand names and product names mentioned in this book are subject to trademark, brand or patent protection and are trademarks or registered trademarks of their respective holders. the use of brand names, product names, common names, trade names, product descriptions etc. even without a particular marking in this work is in no way to be construed to mean that such names may be regarded as unrestricted in respect of trademark and brand protection legislation and could thus be used by anyone.

Cover Image: www.canva.com

Publisher:

Doctorate publications

is an International Publishing house

under Department of Research & Publications

@ eSkilllGrow Virtual University LLCs(regd as per usa govt int'l laws)

USA :

International Regd agent office at Delaware and California, USA

16192.coastal highway city of Lewes.

Administrative Office of Registered agents inc.   90 state street, ste 700 office 40, albany

12207 , county: albany, New York city, USA

e-101 kitchawan rd, yorktown heights, ny 10598, USA

GERMANY:

34/09-a, geschwister-scholl-straße 7, d-39307 genthin, germany

JAPAN:

a-19-21, ihonbashihakozakichō, chūō-ku, tōkyō-to-103-0015, japan.

POLAND:

b-2/45, ul. a. kręglewskiego 11, 61-248-2 poznań, poland

INDIA:
4&5, arpita enclave, karmanghat, hyderabad, telangana

Advanced Pathways - Nurturing Future Computer Science & Engineering Innovators

Doctorate Publications

Index

CHAPTER 1 STRUCTURED PROGRAMMING

A BEGINNERS GUIDE

Instead of using straightforward tests and jumps like the goto statement, which could result in "spaghetti code" that is challenging to understand and maintain, structured programming makes extensive use of subroutines, block structures, and for and while loops. This improves the clarity, quality, and development time of a computer programme.

INTRODUCTION TO COMPUTERS

On a computer, any programming language is implemented. Since their creation to the current day, all computers (regardless of their size and shape) have performed the following 5 fundamental activities. It transforms the unprocessed input data into information that the users may use.

☐ **Inputting**: It entails entering information and commands into the computer system.

☐ **Storing**: The information and instructions are saved for use in initial or subsequent processing as needed.

☐ **Processing**: To transform the recorded data into useable information, arithmetic or logical operations must be applied to it.

☐ **Outputting**: It is the procedure for creating output data for the customer.

☐ **Controlling**: To be successful, the actions need to be carried out in a specific order.

Based on these 5 operations, we can sketch the block diagram of a computer.

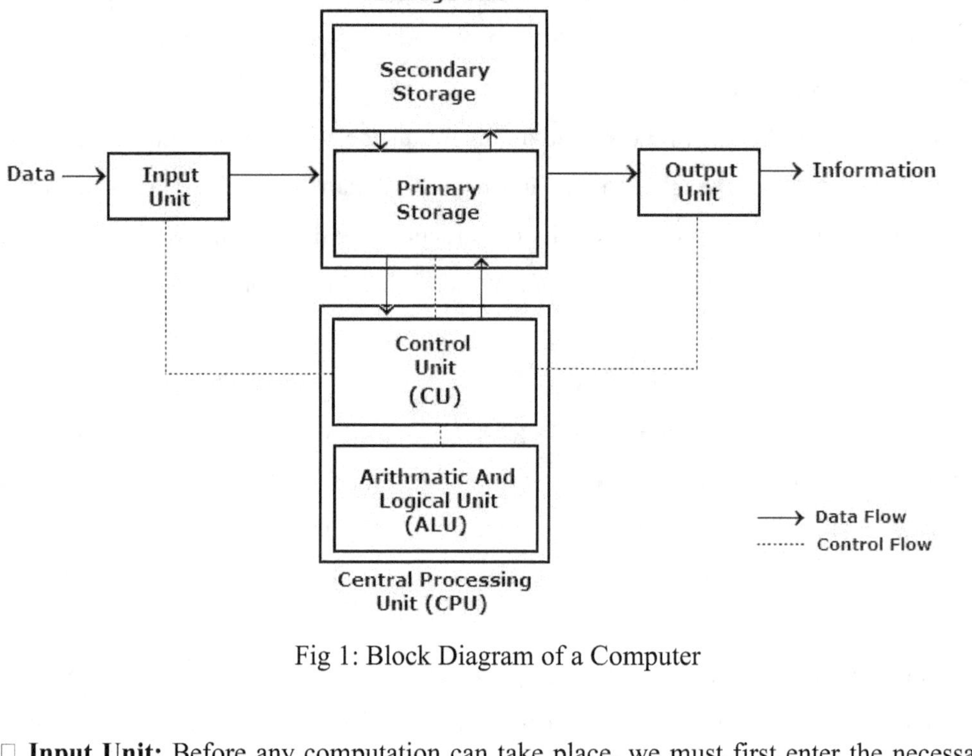

Fig 1: Block Diagram of a Computer

☐ **Input Unit:** Before any computation can take place, we must first enter the necessary data and instructions into the computer system. The input devices complete this duty for us. (Examples include a keyboard, mouse, scanner, digital camera, etc.). This gadget is in charge of connecting the system to the outside world. The accepted data is presented in a human understandable format. It is transformed into a computer-readable format by the input device.

☐ **Storage Unit:** The computer has to store the data and instructions that are entered. Similar to the intermediate results, the final results must also be stored before being sent to the output unit. The storage unit offers a fix for each of these problems. The starting data, the intermediate result, and the final result are all designed to be saved in this storage unit. Primary storage and Secondary storage are both included in this storage unit.

☐ **Primary Storage**: When the computer is turned on, the data is kept in the primary storage, also known as the main memory. The information kept in primary storage is volatile in nature and disappears as soon as the machine is turned off or restarted. Furthermore, because it is made up of pricey semiconductor devices, primary storage often has a low storage capacity.

☐ **Secondary Storage:** The primary memory's storage constraints and volatile nature are handled by the secondary storage, also known as auxiliary storage. Even after the system is turned off, information can still be retained. Basically, it's utilized to store program instructions and data that the computer needs to process later but isn't working on right now.

☐ **Central Processing Unit:** The Control Unit and the Arithmetic Logic Unit are collectively referred to as the Central Processing Unit (CPU). The CPU is the computer's mental center. Like in humans, the brain itself makes the key decisions, and other bodily parts carry out the brain's instructions. The CPU performs all of the significant calculations and comparisons in a computer system similarly. The CPU is in charge of turning on and controlling the operation of other computer system components.

☐ **Arithmetic Logic Unit:** Here, the instructions (arithmetic or logical operations) are really put to use. The primary storage's data and instructions are sent as and when they are needed. The primary store is not used for processing. ALU generates intermediate results, which are momentarily sent back to the primary store until later required. As a result, data may be transited between the primary store and the ALU and back again numerous times before the processing is finished.

☐ **Control Unit:** Although it doesn't really process any data, this unit manages how the entire computer functions. It is in charge of transferring information and commands between the computer's many components. It oversees and plans the operation of every system component. Input/Output devices are also communicated with in order to transfer data or results from the storage units.

☐ **Output Unit:** An output unit's function is the exact opposite of that of an input unit. It accepts computer-generated results in coded form. It transforms these coded results into readable human form. Finally, it uses output devices (such as monitors, printers, projectors, etc.) to show the converted results to the outside world.

Consequently, when we refer to a computer, we really imply two things:

☐ **Hardware:** The entire physical operation of the computer is carried out by this hardware.

☐ **Software:** The hardware is told what to do and how to do it by this software.

The computer system is made up of both the hardware and the software.

System software and application software are further categories for this software.

☐ **System Software:** A group of programmes known as system software are in charge of managing computer resources, operating the computer, and controlling other computer system processes. They serve as a bridge between the computer's hardware and application software.

E.g: Operating System.

Application Software: Application software is a group of programmes created to help users with a specific issue. It enables the end user to perform tasks other than just using the gear.

E.g: Web Browser, Gaming Software, etc.

CHAPTER 2 INTRODUCTION TO PROGRAMMING

Introduction to programming:

Programming, often known as coding, is the process of writing a series of instructions in a language that is understandable by a computer system. Computer languages are also referred to as programming languages. A programme is a collection of instructions created by a computer to carry out a certain activity. Software refers to a collection of extensive programmes. One needs to be knowledgeable about a programming language to create software.

It's necessary to understand the many kinds of languages used by computers before tackling any programming languages. Let's first understand what the programmers' fundamental needs were and what challenges they encountered when writing programmes in that language.

COMPUTER LANGUAGES

A means of communication is language. People typically communicate with one another through language. A language is used to communicate with computers in a similar manner.

Both the user and the machine can understand this language. Every computer language is constrained by the syntax rules of that language, just as every language, including Hindi and English, has its own set of grammatical rules. This syntax controls all communications between the user and the computer system.

Computer languages are broadly classified as:

☐ **Low Level Language**: Low level refers to the notion that it is more similar to a language that a computer can understand.

These are the low-level languages:

☐ **Machine Language**: This is the language that the computer can understand directly (in the form of binary digits, which are made up of 0s and 1s). It is reliant on machines. It's challenging to learn, and writing programmes is even harder.

☐ **Assembly Language**: In order to aid in learning, symbolic codes (referred to as mnemonics) are used in place of the machine codes, which are made up of 0s and 1s. It is the initial stage in improving the structure of programming. Programming in assembly language is less complicated and time-consuming than programming in machine language, and it is also simpler to find and fix faults in assembly language programmes than in machine language programmes. Additionally, it is machine reliant. The computer that will run the programme must be understood by programmers.

☐ **High Level Language:** Since low level language is machine dependant, it necessitates substantial hardware understanding. High level language, which uses everyday English that is simple to comprehend to address any problem, has evolved to get around this limitation.

Programming becomes incredibly straightforward and easy because to high level languages, which are independent of computers. The following list of high-level languages includes:

- BASIC (Beginners All Purpose Symbolic Instruction Code): This general-purpose language is popular and simple to learn. formerly primarily found in microcomputers.

- Common Business Oriented Language (COBOL) is a standardized language used in business applications.

- FORTRAN (Formula Translation): Designed to address issues in mathematics and science. of the most widely used languages in the scientific community.

- C: A structured programming language used for a variety of tasks, including creating games and doing research.

- C++: A well-known, general-purpose object-oriented programming language.

PROGRAMMING LANGUAGE TRANSLATORS

As you are aware, while assembly language is machine dependent and high level language is machine independent, the mnemonics used to represent instructions in assembly language are not directly readable by machines. Programming language instructors are thus utilized to make the computer understand the instructions provided by both languages. They convert the programmers' instructions into a format that the computer can understand and carry out. The different tools that can be used to accomplish this goal are flowing:

☐ **Compiler**: Compiler refers to the software that reads a programme written in high level language and converts it into a machine language equivalent. The source programme is the one created by the programmer in high-level language, while the object programme is the one produced by the compiler following translation.

☐ **Interpreter**: Additionally, it carries out commands written in high-level languages. Although compliers and interpreters share the same objective, which is to translate high level language into binary instructions, they operate in distinct ways. The interpreter takes one statement, translates it, executes it, and then takes the next statement. The compiler transforms the complete source code into a machine-level programme.

☐ **Assembler**: Assemblers are pieces of software that read assembly language programmes and convert them into their machine language equivalents.

☐ **Linker**: A computer programme known as a linker or link editor merges one or more object files produced by a compiler into a single executable file, library file, or additional object file.

CHAPTER 3 INTRODUCTION TO C

Brief History of C:

☐ Dennis Ritchie created the structure-oriented programming language known as C at Bell Laboratories in 1972.

☐ Features of the "B" (Basic Combined computer Language, or BCPL) computer language were adapted into the "C" programming language.

☐ The UNIX operating system was implemented using the C programming language.

☐ Dennis Ritchie and Brian Kernighan published the first edition of "The C Programming Language" in 1978; this book is also referred to as K&R C.

☐ A group to develop a current, thorough description of C was established in 1983 by the American National Standards Institute (ANSI). The resulting definition, known as the "ANSI C" standard, was finished in late 1988.

☐ This new language was given the name "C" since it borrowed many concepts and tenets from the prior language B.

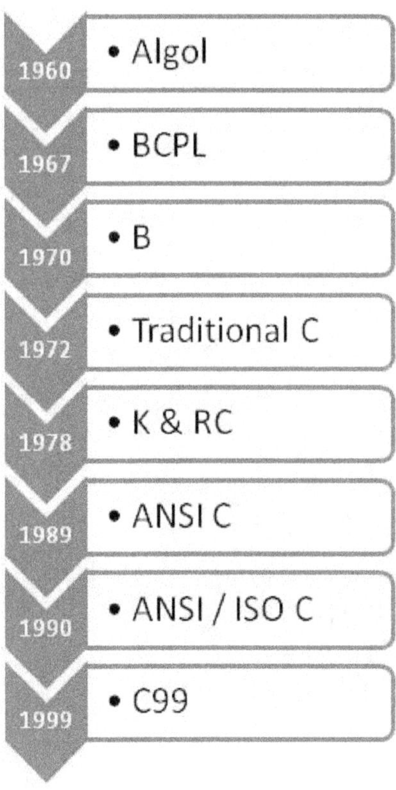

Taxonomy of C Language

WHY IS C POPULAR

☐ It is dependable, clear, and straightforward to use.

☐ C is a condensed, block-based computer language.

☐ Because C is a portable language, programmes created in it can run with little to no modification on several platforms.

☐ One of the most comprehensive collections of operators, including those for calculations and data comparisons, is found in C.

☐ Although the programmer has more latitude when it comes to data storage, the languages do not examine the programmer's data types for accuracy.

WHY TO STUDY C

☐ Early in the 1980s, C was already the language of choice for Unix systems on minicomputers. Since then, it has migrated to mainframes and personal computers (microcomputers).

☐ C is frequently used by software companies to create word processing applications, spreadsheets, compilers, and other products.

☐ Particularly when it comes to writing operating systems, C is a very flexible language.

☐ C contains fifteen levels of precedence, compared to the four or five found in most other languages.

CHARECTERESTICS OF A C PROGRAM

☐ Middle level language

High Level	Middle Level	Low Level
High level languages provide almost everything that the programmer might. need to do as already built into the language.	Middle level languages don't provide all the built-in functions. found in high level languages, but provides all building blocks. that we need to produce the result we want	Low level languages provides nothing. other than access to the machines basic instruction set.
Examples: Java, Python	C, C++	Assembler

☐ Small size - has only 32 keywords.

☐ The C library can be expanded by the end user by using function calls often.

☐ supports loose typing, allowing for the treatment of a character as an integer and vice versa.

☐ Structured language

Structure oriented	Object oriented	Non structure
In this type of language, large programs are divided into small programs called functions	In this type of language, rograms are divided into objects	There is no specific Structure for programming this language
Prime focus is on functions and Procedures that operate on the data	Prime focus is in the data that is being operated and not on the functions or procedures	N/A
Data moves freely around the systems from one function to Another	Data is hidden and cannot be accessed by external functions.	N/A
Program structure follows "Top-Down Approach."	Program structure follows "Bottom-UP Approach"	N/A
Examples: C, Pascal, ALGOL, and Modula-2	C++, JAVA and C# (C sharp)	BASIC, COBOL, FORTRAN

☐ There is easy access to low level (Bit Wise) programming.

☐ Pointer implementation makes significant use of pointers for structures, functions, and memory.

☐ It has high-level constructs.

☐ It can handle low-level activities.

☐ It produces efficient programs.

☐ It can be compiled on a variety of computers.

USES

System applications, which make up the majority of operating systems like Windows, UNIX, and Linux, are developed using the C programming language. Here are some instances of C in use:

☐ Database systems

☐ Graphics packages

☐ Word processors

☐ Spreadsheets

☐ Operating system development

☐ Compilers and Assemblers

☐ Network drivers

☐ Interpreters

STRUCTURE OF A C PROGRAM

A C programmer must adhere to a protocol (set of rules) known as the C program's structure when writing a C programme. The image below depicts the general fundamental structure of a C programme.

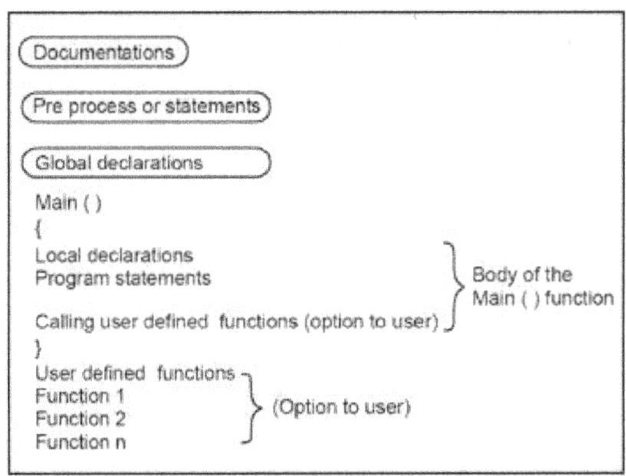

Based on this structure, we can sketch a C program.

Example:

/* This program accepts a number & displays it to the user*/

#include <stdio.h>

void main(void)

```c
{
int number;
printf( "Please enter a number: " );
scanf( "%d", &number );
printf( "You entered %d", number );
return 0;
}
```

Stepwise explanation:

#include

☐ The preprocessor is the component of the compiler that actually extracts your programme from the source file.

☐ #include <stdio.h>

☐ A pre-processor directive is #include. It is a directive to the compiler to cause it to perform a task rather than actually being a component of our programme. In this situation, the system file stdio.h, it instructs the C compiler to include the contents of the file.

☐ Because the filename is encased in > characters, the compiler understands that it is a system file and must be located in a certain location <stdio.h>.

☐ The standard library definition file for all STanDard Input and Output functions is called stdio.h.

☐ The file with the functions we want to utilise specified is called stdio.h, and your programme will almost definitely want to send information to the screen and read data from the keyboard.

☐ We want to use a function called printf. The linker will later tie in the actual printf code.

☐ An include file is identified by the language extension ".h" in the filename.

void

☐ This essentially means that nothing is being said. In this instance, it alludes to the function whose name is shown after.

☐ Void informs the C compiler that an entity is meaningless and does not cause an main error.

☐ The program's sole function in this example is designated as main.

☐ Typically, a C programme consists of several different functions. The programmer gives each of these names, and when the software runs, they are all used to refer to one another.

☐ Since C views the term main as a special case, it will execute this function first, starting the programme at main.

(void)

☐ The keyword void is enclosed in this set of brackets.

☐ The compiler is informed that the main function has no parameters.

☐ A function's parameter provides it with data on which to operate.

{(Brace)}

☐ A brace (or curly bracket) is what this is. As the name suggests, braces are sold in pairs; there must be a close brace for every open brace.

☐ Programme components can be grouped together using braces, which are sometimes known as blocks.

☐ The declaration of a variable that will be utilised within a block may be followed by a series of programme statements.

☐ In this instance, the function main's operational components are enclosed by the braces.

; (semicolon)

☐ The list of variable names and that declaration statement are both concluded with a semicolon.

☐ C programmes use semicolons (";") to separate each statement.

☐ Actually, the character ";" is crucial. It communicates to the compiler the end of a particular statement.

☐ A compiler error will be generated if one of these characters is not present where it is expected to be.

scanf

☐ Other programming languages have printing and reading capabilities as standard features.

☐ Instead, they are defined as standard functions in C, which are a component of the language specification but not the language itself.

☐ There are several functions in the standard input/output library for transferring formatted data; the two we'll use are scanf (scan formatted) and printf (print formatted).

printf

☐ The scanf function's inverse is printf.

☐ It projects text and values onto the screen using data from the programme.

☐ Similar to scanf, it is a feature of all versions of C and is explained in the system file stdio.h.

☐ The format string, which includes text, value descriptions, and formatting instructions, is the first parameter to a printf.

FILES USED IN A C PROGRAM

☐ **Source File:** The program's source code is located in this file. Any file created in C has the.c file extension. The main function and maybe other functions are defined in the file's C source code.

☐ **Header File:** A header file is a file with the.h extension that includes C function declarations and macro definitions and is intended to be shared by many source files.

☐ **Object File:** An object file is a file with the extension.o that contains object code, which is relocatable format computer code that is typically not directly executable. Object files are created by an assembler, compiler, or other language translator and sent through a linker, which commonly assembles the object files into an executable or library.

☐ **Executable File:** The linker creates the binary executable file. The linker joins the different object files to create an executable binary file.

COMPLIATION & EXECUTION OF A C PROGRAM

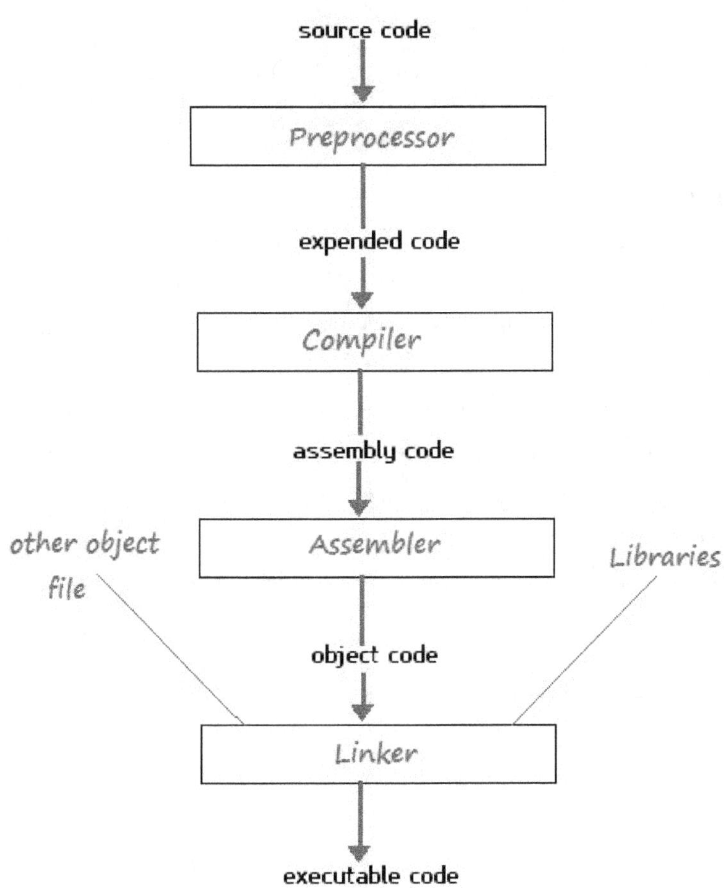

source code
Preprocessor
expended code
Compiler
assembly code
Assembler
object code
other object file
Libraries
Linker
executable code

Elements of c:

There are fundamental components and grammatical principles in every language. Before beginning to programme, we should be familiar with the fundamental building blocks of the language.

Character Set

Speaking the computer's language is necessary for communicating with it. Many different characters can communicate in C.

Character set in C consists of;

Types	Character Set
Lower case	a-z
Upper case	A-Z
Digits	0-9
Special Character	!@#$%^&*
White space	Tab or new lines or space

Keywords

The terms that have previously been defined for the C compiler are known as keywords. Because doing so would attempt to give the term a new meaning, which the computer does not permit, the keywords cannot be utilised as variable names.

In C, there are only 32 possible keywords. For your quick reference, a list of these terms is provided in the image below.

KEYWORDS

auto	do	goto	signed	unsigned
break	double	if	sizeof	void
case	else	int	static	volatile
char	enum	long	struct	while
const	extern	register	switch	
continue	float	return	typeodef	
default	for	short	union	

Identifier

An identifier in the computer language C is a string of alphanumeric characters, where the first character is either an alphabetic letter or an underline and the remaining characters can be any letter of the alphabet, any digit, or the underline.

When naming identifiers, two requirements must be followed.

1. Case matters when using alphabetic characters. There is a difference between using "INDEX" and "index" and between using "Index" and "INDEX" for variables. All three make reference to various variables.

2. According to how C is defined, up to 32 significant characters may be used; most compilers will treat these as such. The compiler will not utilise any more than 32 if they are present.

Data Type

Data types in the C programming language refer to a range of permitted values and the operations that can be carried out on those values. The type of a variable dictates how much storage space it takes up and how the stored bit pattern is interpreted. In C, there are four basic data types: char, int, float, and double. Any single letter can be stored in char; any integer value can be stored in int; any single precision floating point number can be stored in float; and any double precision floating point number can be stored in double. To create more types, we can combine these fundamental kinds with two qualifiers.

There are 2 types of qualifiers-

1. Sign qualifier- signed & unsigned

2. Size qualifier- short & long

The data types in C can be classified as follows:

Type	Storage size	Value range
char		-128 to 127
unsigned char	1 byte	0 to 255
int	2 or 4 bytes	-32,768 to 32,767 or -2,147,483,648to 2,147,483,647
unsigned int	2 or 4 bytes	0 to 65,535 or 0 to 4,294,967,295
Short	2 bytes	-32,768 to 32,767
unsigned short	2 bytes	0 to 65,535
long	4 bytes	-2,147,483,648 to 2,147,483,647
unsigned long	4 bytes	0 to 4,294,967,295

Type	Storage size	Value range	Precision
float	4 bytes	1.2E-38 to 3.4E+38	6 decimal places
double	8 bytes	2.3E-308 to 1.7E+308	15 decimal places
long double	10 bytes	3.4E-4932 to 1.1E+4932	19 decimal places

Constants

A variable is an entity that might vary, as opposed to a constant, which remains constant.

Two broad categories can be used to classify C constants:

- Primary Constants

- Secondary Constants

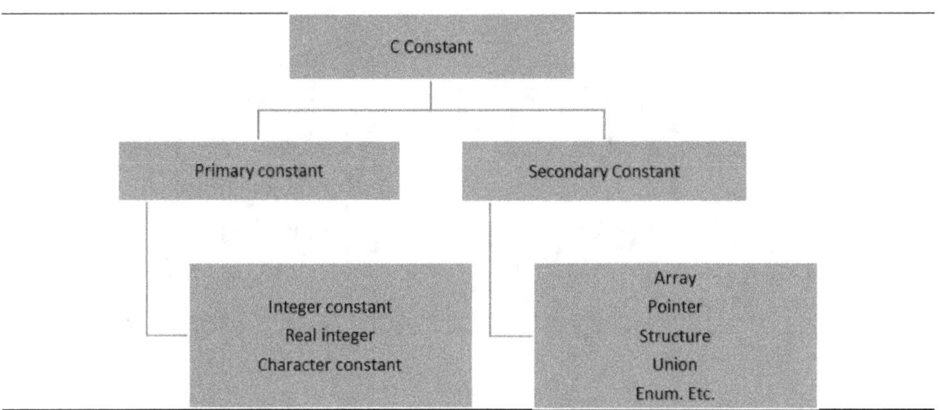

Here, we merely pay attention to the main constant. Certain guidelines have been established for the construction of these various types of constants.

Guidelines for Building Integer Constants:

A minimum of one digit is required for an integer constant.

a) It must not have a decimal point.

b) It can be either positive or negative.

c) If no sign precedes an integer constant it is assumed to be positive.

d) No commas or blanks are allowed within an integer constant.

e) The allowable range for integer constants is -32768to 32767.

Ex: 426, +782,-8000, -7605

Rules for Constructing Real Constants:

Floating Point constants are frequently used to refer to real constants. There are two ways to express real constants: in fractional form and in exponential form.

Real constants given in fractional form must follow certain construction rules.

a)   A real constant must have at least one digit.

b) It must have a decimal point.

c) It could be either positive or negative.

d) Default sign is positive.

e) No commas or blanks are allowed within a real constant.

Ex. +325.34, 426.0, -32.76, -48.5792

Rules for constructing real constants expressed in exponential form:

a) There should be an e between the mantissa and the exponential parts.

b) A positive or negative sign may be present in the mantissa portion.

c) Default sign of mantissa part is positive.

d) A positive or negative integer must make up at least one of the exponent's digits. Sign is positive by default.

e) Real constants have an exponential expression that ranges from -3.4e38 to 3.4e38.

Ex. +3.2e-5, 4.1e8, -0.2e+3, -3.2e-5

Rules for Constructing Character Constants:

a) A single alphabet, one digit, or one unique special symbol wrapped in a single pair of inverted commas is referred to as a character constant.

b) A character constant can have a maximum length of one character.

Ex.: 'M', '6', '+'

CHAPTER 5 VARIABLES

Variables:

Values are stored in names called variables. It can accept several values, but only one at a time. Each variable has a data type associated with it, which determines the possible values for the variable. Simply declare (or create) a new variable whenever you determine your programme requires one, and C will make sure you have access to it. All C variables are declared at the beginning of the relevant code blocks. You must tell C the name and data type of the variable when declaring it.

Syntax - datatype variablename;

Eg:

int page_no;

char grade;

float salary;

long y;

Declaring Variables:

There are two places where you can declare a variable:

• Immediately following a block of code's opening brace (often at the top of a function)

• Before a function name (for instance, before main() in the programme) Take a look at a few examples: Imagine having to remember someone's first, middle, and last initials. The three initials should be stored in three character variables since an initial is obviously a character. You might accomplish that in C by using the following sentence:

```
1.  main()
{
char first, middle, last;
// Rest of program follows
}
2.  main()
{
char first;
char middle;
char last;
```

// Rest of program follows

}

Initialization of Variables

A variable holds undefined value, often known as garbage value, when it is declared. The variables can optionally be given an initial value during the declaration process. Initialization of the variable is what this is known as.

E.g.

int pageno=10;

char grade='A';

float salary= 20000.50;

Expressions

A mix of operators, operands, variables, and function calls make up an expression. A mathematical, logical, or relational expression are all possible. Here are a few phrases:

a+b - arithmetic operation

a>b- relational operation a

== b - logical operation

func (a,b) - function call

4+21

a*(b + c/d)/20

q = 5*2 x =

++q % 3

q > 3

The operands can be constants, variables, or mixtures of the two, as you can see. Subexpressions are larger expressions that are combined to form some expressions. For instance, the sixth example's subexpression is c/d.

Every C expression has a value, which is a crucial characteristic of the language. You must carry out the operations in the sequence specified by operator precedence in order to determine the value.

Statements

A program's fundamental building components are statements. An application is made up of a number of sentences and any appropriate punctuation. An entire instruction to the computer is a statement.

Statements in C are denoted by a semicolon at the conclusion. Legs = 4 is a statement as opposed to Legs = 4 being just an expression (which could be a part of a larger expression).

What attributes do a complete instruction have? First, if you add a semicolon to any expression, C treats it as a statement. Those are what are known as expression statements. C won't object to lines like the following because of this:

8;

3 + 4;

These statements, however, serve no use for your programme and are not truly comprehensible. Statements often invoke functions and update values:

x = 25;

++x;

y = sqrt(x);

Not all full instructions are statements, even though a statement (or at least a logical statement) is a complete command. Think about the following assertion:

x = 6 + (y = 5);

Although it is simply a portion of the statement, the subexpression y = 5 in it is a complete command.

A semicolon is required to denote instructions that are in fact statements because a complete instruction is not always a statement.

Compound Statements (Blocks)

A compound statement, also known as a block, is made up of two or more statements that have been joined together and are enclosed in braces. An illustration of a while statement is provided below:

```
while (years < 100)
{
wisdom = wisdom * 1.05;
printf("%d %d\n", years, wisdom);
years = years + 1;
}
```

Any variable must be declared at the beginning of the block if it is to be used inside the block. Only within the block may variables that are declared inside be used.

CHAPTER 6 INPUT-OUTPUT IN C

Input-output in c:

When we say "input," we mean that we feed a programme with some data. This can be supplied either through the command line or as a file. The built-in functions of the C programming language allow you to read input and pass it along to the programme as needed.

The term "output" refers to the presentation of data on a screen, a printer, or in any other file. A collection of built-in functions in the C programming language are available to output the data on the computer screen.

The most popular functions for taking input and displaying output are printf() and scanf(), respectively. Let's look at an illustration:

```
#include <stdio.h>
int main()
{
//This is needed to run printf() function.
printf("C Programming");  //displays the content inside quotation
return 0;
}
```

Output:

C Programming

Explanation:

☐ Each programme begins with the main() function.

☐ A library function called printf() that displays output only functions if #include<stdio.h> is included at the beginning.

☐ Standard input/output header file stdio.h is used in this case, and the #include command is used to paste the header file's code as needed. Compiler displays error when printf() function is encountered but stdio.h header file cannot be found.

☐ return 0; signifies that the programme ran successfully.

Input- Output of integers in C

```c
#include<stdio.h>
int main()
{
int c=5;
printf("Number=%d",c);
return 0;
}
```
Output
Number=5

There is a conversion format string for integers called "%d" inside the quotation marks of the printf() function. If the conversion format string matches the last argument, which in this case is c, the value of c is shown.

```c
#include<stdio.h>
int main()
{
int c;
printf("Enter a number\n");
scanf("%d",&c);
printf("Number=%d",c);
return 0;
}
```
Output
Enter a number
4
Number=4

To receive human input, use the scanf() function. The user is prompted for an input in this programme, and the value is then placed in variable c. Observe the '&' symbol before c. Value is kept at address c, which is indicated by the symbol & c.

Input- Output of floats in C

```c
#include <stdio.h>
int main()
{
float a;
printf("Enter value: ");
scanf("%f",&a);
printf("Value=%f",a);
return 0;
//%f is used for floats instead of %d
}
```

Output

Enter value: 23.45

Value=23.450000

Conversion format string "%f" is used for floats to take input and to display floating value of a variable.

Input – Output of characters and ASCII code

```c
#include <stdio.h>
int main()
{
char var1;
printf("Enter character: ");
scanf("%c",&var1);
printf("You entered %c.",var1);
return 0;
}
```

Output:

Enter character: g

You entered g.

Conversion format string "%c" is used in case of characters.

ASCII code

In the programme mentioned above, when a character is entered, a numeric value (ASCII value) is instead stored. And that character is displayed when we use "%c" to display that value.

```c
#include <stdio.h>
int main()
{
char var1;
printf("Enter character: ");
scanf("%c",&var1);
printf("You entered %c.\n",var1);
/* \n prints the next line(performs work of enter). */
printf("ASCII value of %d",var1);
return 0;
}
```

Output:

Enter character:

g

103

When the character 'g' is input, the ASCII value 103 is instead kept.

If you merely know the ASCII code, you can show characters. The example that follows demonstrates this.

```c
#include <stdio.h>
int main()
{
int var1=69;
printf("Character of ASCII value 69: %c",var1);
return 0;
}
```

Output

Character of ASCII value 69: E

The ASCII value of 'A' is 65, 'B' is 66 and so on to 'Z' is 90. Similarly ASCII value of 'a' is 97, 'b' is 98 and so on to 'z' is 122.

CHAPTER 7 FORMATTED INPUT-OUTPUT

Formatted input-output:

A specific format for entering and displaying data is available. Improved results display can be achieved by format specifications.

Variations in Output for integer & floats:

```c
#include<stdio.h>
int main()
{
printf("Case 1:%6d\n",9876);
/*  Prints the number right justified within 6 columns  */
printf("Case 2:%3d\n",9876);
/* Prints the number to be right justified to 3 columns but, there are 4 digits so number is not
right justified  */
printf("Case 3:%.2f\n",987.6543);
/* Prints the number rounded to two decimal places */
printf("Case 4:%.f\n",987.6543);
/* Prints the number rounded to 0 decimal place, i.e, rounded to integer */
printf("Case 5:%e\n",987.6543);
/* Prints the number in exponential notation (scientific notation) */
return 0;
}
```

Output:

Case 1: 9876

Case 2:9876

Case 3:987.65

Case 4:988

Case 5:9.876543e+002

Variations in Input for integer and floats:

```c
#include <stdio.h>
int main()
```

```c
{
int a,b;
float c,d;
printf("Enter two intgers: ");
/*Two integers can be taken from user at once as below*/
scanf("%d%d",&a,&b);
printf("Enter intger and floating point numbers: ");
/*Integer and floating point number can be taken at once from user as below*/
scanf("%d%f",&a,&c);
return 0;
}
```

Similarly, any number of inputs can be taken at once from user.

EXERCISE:

1. Which of the following printf() statements will you use to print out the values a and b shown below?

```c
#include<stdio.h>
float a=3.14;
double b=3.14;
```

A. printf("%f %lf", a, b);

B. printf("%Lf %f", a, b);

C. printf("%Lf %Lf", a, b);

D. printf("%f %Lf", a, b);

2. To scan a and b given below, which of the following scanf() statement will you use?

```c
#include<stdio.h>
float a;
double b;
```

A. scanf("%f %f", &a, &b);

B. scanf("%Lf %Lf", &a, &b);

C. scanf("%f %Lf", &a, &b);

D. scanf("%f %lf", &a, &b);

3. For a typical program, the input is taken using.

A. scanf

B. Files

C. Command-line

D. None of the mentioned

4. What is the output of this C code?

```c
#include <stdio.h>
int main()
{
int i = 10, j = 2;
printf("%d\n", printf("%d %d ", i, j));
}
```

A. Compile time error

B. 10 2 4

C. 10 2 2

D. 10 2 5

5. What is the output of this C code?

```c
#include <stdio.h>
int main()
{
int i = 10, j = 3;
printf("%d %d %d", i, j);
}
```

A. Compile time error

B. 10 3

C. 10 3 some garbage value

D. Undefined behavior

6. What is the output of this C code?

```c
#include <stdio.h>
int main()
{
}
int i = 10, j = 3, k = 3;
printf("%d %d ", i, j, k);
```

A. Compile time error

B. 10 3 3

C. 10 3

D. 10 3 somegarbage value

7. The syntax to print a % using printf statement can be done by.

A. %

B. %

C. '%'

D. %%

8. What is the output of this C code?

```c
#include <stdio.h>
int main()
{
int n;
scanf("%d", n);
printf("%d\n", n);
return 0;
}
```

A. Compilation error

B. Undefined behavior

C. Whatever user types

D. Depends on the standard

9. What is the output of this C code?

```c
#include <stdio.h>
int main()
{
short int i;
scanf("%hd", &i);
printf("%hd", i);
return 0;
}
```
A. Compilation error

B. Undefined behavior

C. Whatever user types

D. None of the mentioned

10. In a call to printf() function the format specifier %b can be used to print binary equivalent of an integer.

A. True

B. False

11. Point out the error in the program?
```c
#include<stdio.h>
int main()
{
char ch;
int i;
scanf("%c", &i);
scanf("%d", &ch);
printf("%c %d", ch, i);
return 0;
}
```
A. Error: suspicious char to in conversion in scanf()

B.   Error: we may not get input for second scanf() statement

C. No error

D. None of above

12. Which of the following is NOT a delimiter for an input in scanf?

A. Enter

B. Space

C. Tab

D. None of the mentioned

LECTURE NOTE 2

TWO DIMENSIONAL ARRAYS

Up until now, we have only thought about one-dimensional arrays, or lines of elements. Tables are a common and natural way for data to appear.

e.g spreadsheet, which need a two-dimensional array.

Declaration:

Although two subscripts are used here, the syntax is the same as for a 1-D array.

Syntax:

data_type array_name[rowsize][columnsize];

Rowsize specifies the no.of rows Columnsize specifies the no.of columns.

Example:

int a[4][5];

There are 4 rows and 5 columns in this 2-D array. Here, the array's initial and last components are a[0][0] and a[3][4], respectively, making a total of 4*5=20 elements.

col 0 col 1 col 2 col 3 col 4

row 0 a[0][0] a[0][1] a[0][2] a[0][3] a[0][4] row 1 a[1][0] a[1][1] a[1][2] a[1][3] a[1][4] row 2 a[2][0] a[2][1] a[2][2] a[2][3] a[2][4] row 3 a[3][0] a[3][1] a[3][2] a[3][3] a[3][4]

Initialization:

2-D arrays can be initialized in a way similar to 1-D arrays.

Example:

int m[4][3]={1,2,3,4,5,6,7,8,9,10,11,12};

The values are assigned as follows:

m[0][0]:1 m[0][1]:2 m[0][2]:3

m[1][0]:4 m[1][1]:5 m[3][2]:6 m[2][0]:7 m[2][1]:8 m[3][2]:9 m[3][0]:10 m[3][1]:11 m[3][2]:12

The initialization of group of elements as follows:

int m[4][3]={{11},{12,13},{14,15,16},{17}};

The values are assigned as:

m[0][0]:1 1 m[0][1]:0 m[0][2]:0 m[1][0]:12 m[1][1]:13 m[3][2]:0

m[2][0]:14 m[2][1]:15 m[3][2]:16 m[3][0]:17 m[3][1]:0 m[3][2]:0

Note:

The first dimension in 2-D arrays is optional, while the second dimension must always be present.

Example: int m[][3]={

{1,10},

{2,20,200},

{3},

{4,40,400}};

Since there are 4 roes in the initialization list, the first dimension in this case is 4. Matrix refers to a 2-D array.

Processing:

Two nested for loops are required to parse 2-D arrays. The inner loop shows the columns, while the outer loop shows the rows.

Example:

int a[4][5];

a) Reading values in a for(i=0;i<4;i++)

for(j=0;j<5;j++)

scanf("%d",&a[i][j]);

b) Displaying values of a for(i=0;i<4;i++)

for(j=0;j<5;j++)

printf("%d",a[i][j]);

Example 1:

Write a C program to find sum of two matrices

#include <stdio.h> #include<conio.h>

void main()

```c
{
float a[2][2], b[2][2], c[2][2];
int i,j;
clrscr();
printf("Enter the elements of 1st matrix\n");
/* Reading two dimensional Array with the help of two for loop. If there is an array of 'n' dimension, 'n'
numbers of loops are needed for inserting data to array.*/
for(i=0;i<2;I++)
for(j=0;j<2;j++)
{
scanf("%f",&a[i][j]);
}
printf("Enter the elements of 2nd matrix\n");
for(i=0;i<2;i++)
for(j=0;j<2;j++)
{
scanf("%f",&b[i][j]);
}
/* accessing corresponding elements of two arrays. */ for(i=0;i<2;i++)
for(j=0;j<2;j++)
{
c[i][j]=a[i][j]+b[i][j]; /* Sum of corresponding elements of two arrays. */
}
/* To display matrix sum in order. */ printf("\nSum Of Matrix:"); for(i=0;i<2;++i)
{
for(j=0;j<2;++j)
printf("%f", c[i][j]);
printf("\n");
}
getch();
}
```

Example 2: Program for multiplication of two matrices

```c
#include<stdio.h> #include<conio.h> int main()
{
int i,j,k;
int row1,col1,row2,col2,row3,col3;
int mat1[5][5], mat2[5][5], mat3[5][5];
clrscr();
printf("\n enter the number of rows in the first matrix:");
scanf("%d", &row1);
printf("\n enter the number of columns in the first matrix:");
scanf("%d", &col1);
printf("\n enter the number of rows in the second matrix:");
scanf("%d", &row2);
printf("\n enter the number of columns in the second matrix:");
scanf("%d", &col2);
if(col1 != row2)
{
printf("\n The number of columns in the first matrix must be equal to the number of rows in the second matrix ");
getch(); exit();
}
row3= row1; col3= col3;
printf("\n Enter the elements of the first matrix");
for(i=0;i<row1;i++)
{
for(j=0;j<col1;j++)
scanf("%d",&mat1[i][j]);
}
printf("\n Enter the elements of the second matrix");
for(i=0;i<row2;i++)
{
```

```c
for(j=0;j<col2;j++)
scanf("%d",&mat2[i][j]);
}
for(i=0;i<row3;i++)
{
for(j=0;j<col3;j++)
{
mat3[i][j]=0;
for(k=0;k<col3;k++)
mat3[i][j] +=mat1[i][k]*mat2[k][j];
}
}
printf("\n The elements of the product matrix are"):
for(i=0;i<row3;i++)
{
printf("\n");
for(j=0;j<col3;j++)
printf("\t %d", mat3[i][j]);
}
return 0;
}
```

Output:

Enter the number of rows in the first matrix: 2

Enter the number of columns in the first matrix: 2

Enter the number of rows in the second matrix: 2

Enter the number of columns in the second matrix: 2

Enter the elements of the first matrix

1 2 3 4

Enter the elements of the second matrix

5 6 7 8

The elements of the product matrix are

19 22

43 50

Example 3:

Program to find transpose of a matrix.

```c
#include <stdio.h>
int main()
{
int a[10][10], trans[10][10], r, c, i, j;
printf("Enter rows and column of matrix: ");
scanf("%d %d", &r, &c);
printf("\nEnter elements of matrix:\n");
for(i=0; i<r; i++)
for(j=0; j<c; j++)
{
printf("Enter elements a%d%d: ",i+1,j+1);
scanf("%d", &a[i][j]);
}
/* Displaying the matrix a[][] */ printf("\n Entered Matrix: \n"); for(i=0; i<r; i++)
for(j=0; j<c; j++)
{
printf("%d ",a[i][j]);
if(j==c-1)
printf("\n\n");
}
/* Finding transpose of matrix a[][] and storing it in array trans[][]. */ for(i=0; i<r;i++)
for(j=0; j<c; j++)
{
trans[j][i]=a[i][j];
}
/* Displaying the array trans[][]. */ printf("\nTranspose of Matrix:\n"); for(i=0; i<c;i++)
for(j=0; j<r;j++)
```

```c
{
printf("%d ",trans[i][j]);
if(j==r-1)
printf("\n\n");
} return 0;
}
```

Output:

Enter the rows and columns of matrix: 2 3

Enter the elements of matrix:

Enter elements a11: 1

Enter elements a12: 2

Enter elements a13: 9

Enter elements a21: 0

Enter elements a22: 4

Enter elements a23: 7

Entered matrix:

1 2 9

0 4 7

Transpose of matrix:

1 0

2 4

9 7

Multidimensional Array

Multidimensional arrays are those with more than two dimensions.

Example:

int a[2][3][4];

Here, a stands for two 2-dimensional arrays, each of which has three rows and four columns.

The individual elements are:

a[0][0][0],a[0][0][1],a[0][0][2],a[0][1][0]…………a[0][3][2]

a[1][0][0],a[1][0][1],a[1][0][2],a[1][1][0]…………..a[1][3][2]

the total no. of elements in the above array is 2*3*4=24.

Initialization:

int a[2][4][3]={

{

{1,2,3},

{4,5},

{6,7,8},

{9}

},

{

{10,11},

{12,13,14},

{15,16},

{17,18,19}

}

}

The values of elements after this initialization are as:

a[0][0][0]:1 a[0][0][1]:2 a[0][0][2]:3 a[0][1][0]:4 a[0][1][1]:5 a[0][1][2]:0

a[0][2][0]:6 a[0][2][1]:7 a[0][2][2]:8

a[0][3][0]:9 a[0][3][1]:0 a[0][3][2]:0

a[1][0][0]:10 a[1][0][1]:11 a[1][0][2]:0 a[1][1][0]:12 a[1][1][1]:13 a[1][1][2]:14 a[1][2][0]:15

a[1][2][1]:16 a[1][2][2]:0 a[1][3][0]:17 a[1][3][1]:18 a[1][3][2]:19

Note:

The last subscript varies most frequently and the first subscript fluctuates least frequently when multidimensional arrays are initialised.

Example:

#include<stdio.h>

main()

```c
{
int d[5]; int i;
for(i=0;i<5;i++)
{
d[i]=i;
}
for(i=0;i<5;i++)
{
printf("value in array %d\n",a[i]);
}
}
```

pictorial representation of d will look like

| d[0] | d[1] | 1 | 2 | 3 | 4 |

| d[2] | d[3] |

d[4] 0

CHAPTER 8 ARRAYS USING FUNCTIONS

1-d arrays using functions Passing individual array elements to a function

Like other straightforward variables, we can send specific array elements as arguments to a function.

Example:

```c
#include<stdio.h> void check(int); void main()
{
int a[10],i;
clrscr();
printf("\n enter the array elements:"); for(i=0;i<10;i++)
{
scanf("%d",&a[i]);
check(a[i]);
}
void check(int num)
{
if(num%2==0)
printf("%d is even\n",num); else
printf("%d is odd\n",num);
}
```

Output:

enter the array elements:

1 2 3 4 5 6 7 8 9 10

1 is odd

2 is even

3 is odd

4 is even

5 is odd

6 is even

7 is odd

8 is even

9 is odd

10 is even

Example:

C program to pass a single element of an array to function

```
#include <stdio.h>
void display(int a)
{
printf("%d",a);
}
int main()
{
int c[]={2,3,4};
display(c[2]); //Passing array element c[2] only.
return 0;
}
```

Output:

2 3 4

Passing whole 1-D array to a function

The formal arguments should be declared as an array variable of the same type. We can pass a whole array as an actual argument to a function.

Example:

```
#include<stdio.h>
main()
{
int i, a[6]={1,2,3,4,5,6};
func(a);
printf("contents of array:"); for(i=0;i<6;i++)
printf("%d",a[i]);
printf("\n");
```

```c
}
func(int val[])
{
int sum=0,i;
for(i=0;i<6;i++)
{
val[i]=val[i]*val[i];
sum+=val[i];
}
printf("the sum of squares:%d", sum);
}
```

Output:

contents of array: 1 2 3 4 5 6 the sum of squares: 91

Example2:

To pass an array containing a person's age to a function, create a C programme. The average age should be determined by this function and displayed in the main function.

```c
#include <stdio.h>
float average(float a[]);
int main()
{
float avg, c[]={23.4, 55, 22.6, 3, 40.5, 18};
avg=average(c); /* Only name of array is passed as argument. */
printf("Average age=%.2f",avg);
return 0;
}
float average(float a[])
{
int i;
float avg, sum=0.0;
for(i=0;i<6;++i)
```

```c
{
sum+=a[i];
}
avg =(sum/6);
return avg;
}
```

Output:

Average age= 27.08

Solved Example:

1. Create a programme to locate the greatest n-bit value in an array.

```c
#include <stdio.h>
#include<conio.h>
void main()
{
int array[100], maximum, size, c, location = 1; clrscr();
printf("Enter the number of elements in array\n");
scanf("%d", &size);
printf("Enter %d integers\n", size);
for (c = 0; c < size; c++)
scanf("%d", &array[c]);
maximum = array[0];
for (c = 1; c < size; c++)
{
if (array[c] > maximum)
{
maximum = array[c];
location = c+1;
}
}
printf("Maximum element is present at location %d and it's value is %d.\n", location, maximum);
```

getch();

}

Output:

Enter the number of elements in array

5

Enter 5 integers

2

4

7

9

1

Maximum element is present at location 4 and it's value is 9

2. Create a programme to enter an n-digit number. These digits can be used to create a number.

```c
# include<stdio.h> #include<conio.h> #include<math.h>
void main()
{
int number=0,digit[10], numofdigits,i; clrscr();
printf("\n Enter the number of digits:"); scanf("%d", &numofdigits); for(i=0;i<numofdigits;i++)
{
printf("\n Enter the %d th digit:", i);
scanf("%d",&digit[i]);
} i=0;
while(i<numofdigits)
{
number= number + digit[i]* pow(10,i)
i++;
}
printf("\n The number is : %d",number);
getch();
}
```

Output:

Enter the number of digits: 3

Enter the 0th digit: 5

Enter the 1th digit: 4

Enter the 2th digit: 3

The number is: 543

3. Matrix addition:

```c
#include <stdio.h>
#include<conio.h>
void main()
{
int m, n, c, d, first[10][10], second[10][10], sum[10][10]; clrscr();
printf("Enter the number of rows and columns of matrix\n");
scanf("%d%d", &m, &n);
printf("Enter the elements of first matrix\n");
for ( c = 0 ; c < m ; c++ ) for ( d = 0 ; d < n ; d++ )
scanf("%d", &first[c][d]);
printf("Enter the elements of second matrix\n");
for ( c = 0 ; c < m ; c++ ) for ( d = 0 ; d < n ; d++ )
scanf("%d", &second[c][d]);
for ( c = 0 ; c < m ; c++ )
for ( d = 0 ; d < n ; d++ )
sum[c][d] = first[c][d] + second[c][d];
printf("Sum of entered matrices:-\n");
for ( c = 0 ; c < m ; c++ )
{
for ( d = 0 ; d < n ; d++ )
printf("%d\t", sum[c][d]);
printf("\n");
}
```

getch();

}

Output:

Enter the number of rows and columns of matrix

2

2

Enter the elements of first matrix

1 2

3 4

Enter the elements of second matrix

5 6

2 1

Sum of entered matrices:- 6 8

5 5

Exercise

1. Can a programme compute the sum of an array's elements?

2. Create a programme that prints a histogram using an array?

3. Create a dice-rolling programme utilising an array rather than a switch?

4. Using bubble sort to order an array?

5. Create a binary search programme using an array.

6. Create a programme that switches the array's biggest and smallest numbers.

7. Create a programme to fill a square matrix with the values 0, 1, and -1 on the upper right triangle and the diagonals.

8. Create a programme to read a 2x2x2 array and display it.

9. Create a programme to determine how many elements in the array are duplicates.

10. Determine the average, variance, and standard deviation of an array of integers by computing their sum and values.

11. Create a programme that scans a matrix and sums the items above the primary diagonal.

12. Create a programme to calculate XA + YB where X=2, and Y=3 and A and B are matrices.

CHAPTER 9 FUNDAMENTALS OF STRINGS

Fundamentals of Strings:

A string is a collection of characters that are handled as one entity. A string can contain letters, numbers, and a number of special characters like +, -, *, /, and $. In C, string literals and string constants are denoted by double quotation marks like in the example below:

"1000 Main Street" (a street address)

"(080)329-7082" (a telephone number)

"Kalamazoo, New York" (a city)

In the C programming language, strings are kept in an array of the char type with the null character '0' at the end.

In order to account for the '0' null termination character, we must increase the size of the string array by one.

Syntax:

char fname[4];

The above statement declares a string with a maximum length of three characters, called frame. It can also be indexed in the same way as a typical array.

character	t	w	o	\0
ASCII code	116	119	41	0

Generalized syntax is:-

char str[size];

The string may be declared in this fashion since the last character would be the null character, allowing us to put size-1 characters in the array. The maximum number of characters that can be stored in char mesg[10]; is 9.

We can use this method to print a string from a variable, like the four name string from earlier.

e.g., printf("First name:%s",fname);

More than one variable can be inserted. Conversion guidelines %s is used to insert a string, after which we print each %s of the string.

An array of characters makes up a string. It can therefore be indexed like an array.

char ourstr[6] = "EED";

– ourstr[0] is 'E'

– ourstr[1] is 'E'

– ourstr[2] is 'D'

– ourstr[3] is '\0'

– ourstr[4] is '\0' – ourstr[5] is '\0'

'E'	'E'	'D'	\0	'\0'	'\0'

Reading strings:

If we declare a string by writing char str[100];

then str can be read from the user by using three ways;

1. Using scanf() function

2. Using gets() function

3. Using getchar(), getch(), or getche() function repeatedly

By writing scanf("%s",str"), the string can be read using the scanf() function.

The biggest drawback of the scanf() function is that it quits as soon as it encounters a blank space, despite the fact that its syntax is well-known and simple to use. For instance, str will only include Hello if the user types Hello World. This is due to the scanf() function's termination of the string at the first instance of a blank space.

Example:

char str[10];

printf("Enter a string\n");

scanf("%s",str);

The gets() function is the next technique for reading a string. The string can be read by writing gets(str); the method gets() fixes scanf()'s shortcomings. The initial address of the string that will contain the input is passed to the gets() function. The gets() function automatically ends the string that was entered with the null character.

Example:

char str[10];

printf("Enter a string\n");

gets(str);

If an ending character is not encountered, the string can alternatively be read by continuously executing getchar() to read a series of single characters while simultaneously storing it in a character array as follows:

```c
int i=0;
char str[10],ch;
getchar(ch);
while(ch!='\0')
{
str[i]=ch; // store the read character in str
i++;
getch(ch); // get another character
}
str[i]='\0'; // terminate str with null character
```

Writing string

The string can be displayed on screen using three ways:

1. Using printf() function
2. Using puts() function
3. Using putchar() function repeatedly

The string can be displayed using pintf() by writing printf("%s",str);

Along with %s, we may also employ width and precision specifications. The precision provides the maximum number of characters to be displayed, while the width specifies the minimum output field width. Example:

printf("%5.3s",str);

In a field with a total of five characters, this statement would only print the first three; these three characters would also be right justified within the available width.

The puts() function is the following way to write a string. You may see the string by writing:

puts(str);

It uses the newline character ('n') to end the line. If there is a mistake, it produces an EOF(-1); otherwise, it returns a positive number.

The string can then be created by repeatedly executing the putchar() function to output a series of single characters.

int i=0;
char str[10];

```c
while(str[i]!='\0')
{
putchar(str[i]); // print the character on the screen
i++;
}
```

Example:

Read and display a string

```c
#include<stdio.h>
#include<conio.h>
void main()
{
char str[20];
clrscr();
printf("\n Enter a string:\n"); gets(str);
scanf("The string is:\n"); puts(str);
getch();
}
```

Output:

Enter a string: vssut burla

The string is: vssut burla

CHAPTER 10 COMMON FUNCTIONS IN STRING

Common functions in string:

Type	Method	Description
char	strcpy(s1, s2)	Copy string
char	strcat(s1, s2)	Append string
int	strcmp(s1, s2)	Compare 2 strings
int	strlen(s)	Return string length
char	strchr(s, int c)	Find a character in string
char	strstr(s1, s2)	Find string s2 in string s1

strcpy():

One string can be copied onto another string using it. The second string's content gets copied over to the first string's content.

Syntax:

strcpy (string 1, string 2);

Example:

char mystr[10];

mystr = "Hello"; // Error! Illegal !!! Because we are assigning the value to mystr which is not possible in case of an string. We can only use "=" at declarations of C-String.

strcpy(mystr, "Hello");

It sets value of mystr equal to "Hello".

strcmp():

It is utilised to compare the two strings' contents. If there is a discrepancy, the difference in ASCII values between the first occurrence of two distinct characters will show up.

Syntax:

int strcmp(string 1, string 2);

Example:

char mystr_a[10] = "Hello";

char mystr_b[10] = "Goodbye";

– mystr_a == mystr_b; // NOT allowed! The correct way is

if (strcmp(mystr_a, mystr_b))

printf ("Strings are NOT the same.");

else

printf("Strings are the same.");

Here, it will determine that H and G have the ASCII values 72 and 71, respectively, and return the difference of 1.

strcat():

Concatenating, or combining, the contents of two strings, is what it is used for.

Syntax:

strcat(string 1, string 2);

Example:

char fname[30]={"bob"};

char lname[]={"by"};

printf("%s", strcat(fname,lname));

Output:

bobby.

strlen():

It is used to return the length of a string.

Syntax:

int strlen(string);

Example:

char fname[30]={"bob"}; int length=strlen(fname); It will return 3

strchr():

It is used to locate a character within the string and returns the position where the character appears for the first time.

Syntax:

strchr(cstr);

Example:

char mystr[] = "This is a simple string"; char pch = strchr(mystr,'s');

The output of pch is mystr[3]

strstr():

It is used to determine whether a string exists inside of another string and returns the string's initial starting index.

Syntax:

strstr(cstr1, cstr2);

Example:

Char mystr[]="This is a simple string"; char pch = strstr(mystr, "simple");

here pch will point to mystr[10]

• String input/output library functions

Function prototype	Function description
int getchar(void);	Inputs the next character from the standard input and returns it as integer
int putchar(int c);	Prints the character stored in c and returns it as an integer
int puts(char s);	Prints the string s followed by new line character. Returns a non-zero integer if possible or EOF if an error occurs
int sprint(char s, char format,….)	Equivalent to printf,except the output is stored in the array s instead of printed in the screen. Returns the no.of characters written to s, or EOF if an error occurs
int sprint(char s, char format,….)	Equivalent to scanf, except the input is read from the array s rather than from the keyboard. Returns the no.of items successfully read by the function , or EOF if an error occurs

NOTE:

Character arrays are known as strings.

Self-review exercises:

1. In each of the following programme portions, locate the issue and describe how to fix it:

• char s[10];

• strcpy(s,"hello",5);

• prinf("%s\n",s);

• printf("%s",'a');

• char s[12]; strcpy(s,"welcome home");

• If (strcmp(string 1, sring 2))

{

printf("the strings are equal\n");

}

2. Give examples of two distinct ways to initialise a character array with the vowel string "AEIOU"?

3. Create a programme that transforms a string into an integer?

Create a programme that can accept a word and a line of text. Show the number of times that word appears in the text?

5. Create a programme that would read a word and rewrite its letters in the alphabet.

6. Create a programme that will add a word to the text before a specified word.

7. Create a programme that counts the characters, words, and lines in the provided text.

CHAPTER 11 STRUCTURE AND UNION

Definition

A user-defined data type called a structure can be used to group together relevant pieces of information. Each variable in a structure has a name that may be used to choose it from the structure. These variables are of various data kinds. Structure is another user-defined data type that is accessible in C programming and lets you to combine data items of different kinds. C arrays allow you to construct types of variables that can hold numerous data items of the same kind.

Records are represented by structures, Imagine you wish to manage the books you have in a library. You might want to keep track of each book's following characteristics:

• Title

• Author

• Subject

• Book ID

Structure Declaration

It is declared by using the term struct and the structure's name. The structure's variables are stated within the structure.

Example:

Struct struct-name

{

data_type var-name;

data_type var-name;

};

Structure Initialization

Initialising a structure is the process of assigning constants to its members.

Syntax:

struct struct_name

{

data _type member_name1;

data _type member_name2;

} struct_var={constant1,constant2};

Accessing the Members of a structure

Typically, the '.' operator is used to retrieve a structural member variable.

Syntax: strcut_var. member_name;

To choose a specific structure member, use the dot operator. We write stud.roll=01 to give the various data elements of the structural variable stud a value.

stud.name="Rahul";

To input values for data members of the structure variable stud, can be written as,

scanf("%d",&stud.roll);

scanf("'%s",&stud.name);

To print the values of structure variable stud, can be written as:

printf("%s",stud.roll);

printf("%f",stud.name);

QUESTIONS

1. Create a programme that reads and displays employee information using structures.

2. To read, display, add, and subtract two complex numbers, write a programme.

3. Create a programme that allows you to enter two points and determine their distance from one another.

A nested structure is a structure that has another structure as one of its components, or a structure inside of another structure. It is best to define each structure individually before grouping them into high-level structures.

4. Create a programme utilising nested structures to read and display the information of each student in the class.

Passing Structures through pointers

A variable that stores the address of a structure is called a pointer to a structure. The following syntax can be used to declare a pointer to a structure:

strcut struct_name *ptr;

We would write ptr_stud=&stud to assign the address of the stud to the pointer using the address operator (&). The (->) operator is used to access the structure's members.

for example

Ptr_stud->name=Raj;

SELF REFERENTIAL STRUCTURE

Structures that contain a reference to data of the same type as the structure are said to be self-referential.

Example

struct node

{

int val;

struct node*next;

};

Pointers to Structures

Similar to how you define a pointer to any other variable, you can define pointers to structures as follows:

struct books *struct_pointer;

The address of a structural variable can now be stored in the pointer variable that was previously defined. Place the & operator before the structure's name as shown below to determine the location of a structure variable:

struct_pointer = &book1;

Using a pointer to that structure, you must use the -> operator as shown below to access the members of that structure:

struct_pointer->title;

1. Create a programme that can add, subtract, and show two times that are defined by the hour, minute, and second values.

2. To initialise the structure's members, create a programme using a pointer to the structure. Print the information about the pupils using functions.

3. Create a programme that reads and displays student data using an array of pointers to a structure.

CHAPTER 13 UNION

Union:

Information can only be kept in one field at a time in a union, which is a collection of variables with various data types. In C, there is a unique data type called a union that lets you store many data types in the same memory address. A union can have numerous members, but only one of those members can ever have a value present. Unions offer a practical method for serving many purposes with the same memory location.

Declaring Union

union union-name

{

data_type var-name;

data_type var-name;

};

Each member definition is a typical variable definition, such as int i, float f, or any other acceptable variable definition, and the union tag is optional. It is optional to specify one or more union variables before the last semicolon at the end of the union specification. This is how a union type called Data, which contains the three members i, f, and str, would be defined. Now, a Data type variable can hold a string of characters, a floating-point value, or an integer. This implies that different types of data can be stored in the same memory area using a single variable. Depending on your needs, you can utilise any built-in or user-defined data types inside a union.

A union will have enough space in its memory to accommodate its largest member. For instance, in the example above, the data type will take up 20 bytes of memory space because this is the maximum amount of space that a character string can use. The example that will show the total amount of memory that the aforementioned union has used is as follows:

Accessing a Member of a Union

#include <stdio.h> #include <string.h> union Data

{

int i;

float f;

char str[20];

```c
};
int main( )
{
union Data data;
data.i = 10;
data.f = 220.5;
strcpy( data.str, "C Programming");
printf( "data.i : %d\n", data.i);
printf( "data.f : %f\n", data.f);
printf( "data.str : %s\n", data.str); return 0;
}
```

To contact a union member, use the dot operator. The period that is coded between the name of the union variable and the union member that we want to access is the member access operator. To define variables of the union type, use the union keyword. Here's an illustration of how to use union:

Exercises:

1. Create a programme to define a union and a structure with the same members in both cases. Print the sizes of the structure and union variables using the sizeof operator, then explain the outcome.

2. Create a programme to describe a hotel structure with each member's name, address, grade, number of rooms, and room rates. Create a method to output the hotel names for a specific grade. Create a function that prints the names of hotels with room rates below the required amount as well.

CHAPTER 13 POINTERS

Pointers:

A variable that holds the address of a variable is called a pointer. Pointers are frequently used in C, in part because they are occasionally the only way to express a computation and in part because they typically produce more compact and efficient code than is possible using alternative methods. This chapter examines and demonstrates how to take use of the link between pointers and arrays.

Pointers and the goto statement have been grouped together as a fantastic technique to write programmes that are tough to understand. This is undoubtedly the case when they are used carelessly, and pointers that point in unexpected directions are simple to make. But pointers can also be utilised to achieve clarity and simplicity if they are used with discipline. We shall attempt to illustrate this aspect.

The key modification to ANSI C is the clarification of the guidelines for manipulating pointers, thereby enforcing what good programmers already do and what excellent compilers already do. In addition, the appropriate type for a generic pointer has been changed from char * to void * (reference to void).

Pointers and Addresses

Let's start with a condensed representation of how memory is structured. A typical machine comprises a collection of memory cells with successive numbers or addresses that can be operated on individually or collectively. Any byte can function as a character, a pair of one-byte cells can be used to represent a short integer, and four adjacent bytes can be used to represent a long. A pointer is a collection of cells that can store an address (often two or four). We could therefore describe the scenario in the following manner if c is a char and p is a pointer that points to it:

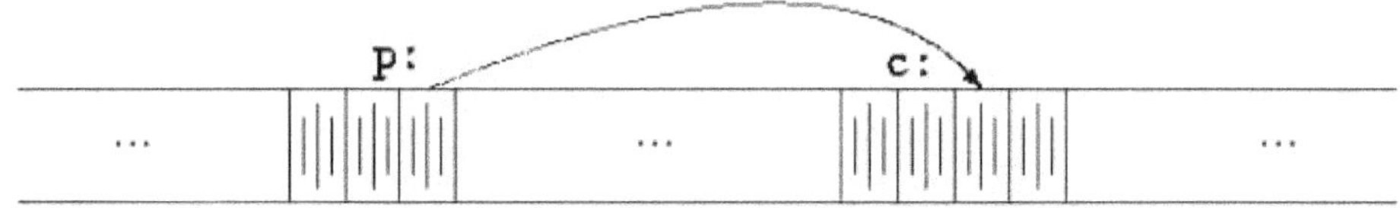

The unary operator &gives the address of an object, therefore the sentence p = &c; assigns the address of c to the variable p, and p is said to "point to" c. Only variables and array elements that are in memory are applicable to the &operator. Expressions, constants, and register variables are not subject to it.

When used with a pointer, the unary operator *, also known as the indirection or dereferencing operator, allows access to the object that the pointer refers to. Assume that ip is a reference to an int and that x and y are both integers. This fictitious sequence demonstrates the declaration of a pointer and the use of &and *:

int x = 1, y = 2, z[10];

int *ip;

ip = &x;

y = *ip;

*ip = 0;

ip = &z[0];

We have been watching the proclamation of x, y, and z the entire time. The expression *ipis an int, according to the declaration of the pointer ip. int *ip;, which is meant to serve as a mnemonic. A variable's declaration replicates the syntax of any possible expressions in which it might appear. The same logic is true for function declarations. For example,

double *dp, atof(char *);

claims that the values of the expressions *dp and atof(s) are double, and that the argument to atof is a pointer to a char.

The fact that every pointer links to a particular data type implies that a pointer is restricted to pointing to a certain sort of object. If the number ippoints to, then *ipcan occur in any situation where x could, so

*ip = *ip + 10;

increments *ip by 10.

The assignment y = *ip + 1 takes whatever ippoints at, adds 1, and assigns the result to y, whereas *ip += 1 increases what ippoints to, as do ++*ip and (*ip)++. Unary operators * and &bind more tightly than arithmetic operators.

In this final example, brackets are required because, without them, unary operators like * and ++ associate right to left, which would lead the expression to increment ip rather than the value it points to. Pointers can also be utilised without dereferencing because they are variables. To make iq point to whatever ippointed to, for instance, if iq is another pointer to int, iq = ip transfers the contents of ipinto iq.

Pointers and Function Arguments

There is no direct mechanism for the called function to change a variable in the calling function since C delivers parameters to functions by value. For instance, a sorting algorithm might use the swap function to swap two out-of-order parameters. It is insufficient to just write swap(a, b);

where the swap function is defined as

```
void swap(int x, int y)
{
int temp;
temp = x;
x = y;
y = temp;
}
```

Swap cannot change the inputs a and b in the function that called it due to call by value. The a and b copies are switched in the function above. The caller programme must pass pointers to the values that need to be altered in order to achieve the desired result:

```
swap(&a, &b);
```

&a is a pointer to a because the operator & generates the address of a variable. The operands are accessed indirectly through the parameters, which are defined as pointers in the swap function itself.

```
void swap(int *px, int *py) /* interchange *px and *py */
{
int temp;
temp = *px;
*px = *py;
*py = temp;
}
```

A function can access and modify items in the function that called it by using pointer parameters. Take the function getint, for instance, which converts free-format input by dividing a stream of characters into integer values, one integer per call. When there is no more input, getint must notify the end of the file and return the value it discovered. Since any value used for EOF could also be the value of an input integer, these values must be returned via different pathways.

One approach is to use a pointer argument to keep the converted integer back in the calling function while having getint return the end of file status as the function value. This is the method that scanfas use well.

By using getint calls, the following loop populates an array with integers:

```
int n, array[SIZE], getint(int *);

for (n = 0; n < SIZE &&getint(&array[n]) != EOF; n++);
```

Each call increments n and sets array[n] to the following integer in the input. Keep in mind that you must supply getint with the address of array[n]. Without this, getint is unable to return the converted integer to the caller.

Our implementation of getintreturns EOF for end of file, zero if the following input does not contain a number, and a positive value if it does.

```
#include <ctype.h>

int getch(void);

void ungetch(int);

int getint(int *pn)

{

int c, sign;

while (isspace(c = getch()));

if (!isdigit(c) && c != EOF && c != '+' && c != '-')

{

ungetch(c); return 0;

}

sign = (c == '-') ? -1 : 1;

if (c == '+' || c == '-')

c = getch();

for (*pn = 0; isdigit(c), c = getch())

*pn = 10 * *pn + (c - '0');

*pn *= sign;

if (c != EOF)

ungetch(c);

return c;
```

}

Getint uses *pnis as a regular int variable throughout. Additionally, we've utilised getch and ungetch so that the final character that needs to be read can be returned to the input.

int x = 1, y = 2, z[10];

int *ip;

ip = &x;

y = *ip;

*ip = 0;

ip = &z[0];

We have been watching the proclamation of x, y, and z the entire time. The expression *ipis an int, according to the declaration of the pointer ip. int *ip;, which is meant to serve as a mnemonic. A variable's declaration replicates the syntax of any possible expressions in which it might appear. The same logic is true for function declarations. For instance, double *dp, atof(char *); indicates that the arguments to atof are pointers to chars and that the values of *dp and atof(s) in an expression are both doubles.

The fact that every pointer links to a particular data type implies that a pointer is restricted to pointing to a certain sort of object. If the number ippoints to, then *ipcan occur in any situation where x could, so

*ip = *ip + 10;

increments *ip by 10.

The assignment y = *ip + 1 takes whatever ippoints at, adds 1, and assigns the result to y, whereas *ip += 1 increases what ippoints to, as do ++*ip and (*ip)++. Unary operators * and &bind more tightly than arithmetic operators.

In this final example, brackets are required because, without them, unary operators like * and ++ associate right to left, which would lead the expression to increment ip rather than the value it points to. Pointers can also be utilised without dereferencing because they are variables. To make iq point to whatever ippointed to, for instance, if iq is another pointer to int, iq = ip transfers the contents of ipinto iq.

Pointers and Function Arguments

There is no direct mechanism for the called function to change a variable in the calling function since C delivers parameters to functions by value. For instance, a sorting algorithm might use the swap function to swap two out-of-order parameters. It is insufficient to just write swap(a, b);

where the swap function is defined as

void swap(int x, int y)

{

int temp;

temp = x;

x = y;

y = temp;

}

Swap cannot change the inputs a and b in the function that called it due to call by value. The a and b copies are switched in the function above. The calling programme must pass pointers to the values that need to be altered in order to achieve the desired result swap(&a, &b); Since the operator & produces the address of a variable, &a is a pointer to a. The operands are accessed indirectly through the parameters, which are defined as pointers in the swap function itself.

void swap(int *px, int *py) /* interchange *px and *py */

{

int temp;

temp = *px;

*px = *py;

*py = temp;

}

A function can access and modify items in the function that called it by using pointer parameters. Take the function getint, for instance, which converts free-format input by dividing a stream of characters into integer values, one integer per call. When there is no more input, getint must notify the end of the file and return the value it discovered. Since any value used for EOF could also be the value of an input integer, these values must be returned via different pathways.

One approach is to use a pointer argument to keep the converted integer back in the calling function while having getint return the end of file status as the function value. This is the method that scanfas use well.

By using getint calls, the following loop populates an array with integers:

```c
int n, array[SIZE], getint(int *);
for (n = 0; n < SIZE &&getint(&array[n]) != EOF; n++);
```

Each call increments n and sets array[n] to the following integer in the input. Keep in mind that you must supply getint with the address of array[n]. Without this, getint is unable to return the converted integer to the caller.

Our implementation of getintreturns EOF for end of file, zero if the following input does not contain a number, and a positive value if it does.

```c
#include <ctype.h>
int getch(void);
void ungetch(int);
int getint(int *pn)
{
int c, sign;
while (isspace(c = getch()));
if (!isdigit(c) && c != EOF && c != '+' && c != '-')
{
ungetch(c); return 0;
}
sign = (c == '-') ? -1 : 1;
if (c == '+' || c == '-')
c = getch();
for (*pn = 0; isdigit(c), c = getch())
*pn = 10 * *pn + (c - '0');
*pn *= sign;
if (c != EOF)
ungetch(c);
return c;
}
```

*pnis utilised as an ordinary int variable throughout getint. In order to push the one additional character that needs to be read back onto the input, we have additionally used getchand ungetch.

CHAPTER 14 Pointers and Arrays

Pointers and Arrays:

Pointers and arrays in the C programming language have a close link that calls for their discussion together. Pointers can be used to do every action that array subscripting can. The pointer version will typically be quicker but, at least to the layman, a little more difficult to comprehend. The statement int a[10]; designates a block of 10 consecutive objects with the names a[0], a[1],., and a[9] that make up an array of size 10. The i-th element of the array is indicated by the notation a[i]. The assignment pa = &a[0]; sets pa to point to element zero of a, i.e., pa contains the address of a[0], if pa is a pointer to an integer specified as int *pa. The task x =*pa; will now copy the data from a[0] into x.

If an array's element pa points to a specific one, then pa+1 points to the element after it, pa+i points to the element after pa, and pa-i points to the element before. As a result, if pa points to a[0], *(pa+1) denotes the information in a[1,] pa+iis the address of a[i], and *(pa+i) denotes the information in a[i]. These statements are accurate regardless of the kind or quantity of variables in array a. All pointer arithmetic, including "adding 1 to a pointer," means that pa+1 points to the object after pa, and pa+i points to the i-th item after pa. Pointer arithmetic and indexing closely resemble one other. The address of array element zero is, by definition, the value of a variable or expression of type array. As a result, when pa = &a[0], both pa and a have the same value. The assignment pa=&a[0] can also be written as pa = a since the name of an array is a synonym for the position of the first element.

At first glance, it may seem more unexpected that a reference to a[i] can alternatively be expressed as *(a+i). C immediately changes a[i] to *(a+i) after evaluating it; the two forms are identical. It follows that &a[i] and a+iare likewise equivalent when the operator &is applied to both sides of this equivalence because a+iis the address of the i-th element after a. The flip side of this is that expressions may use pa with a subscript if it is a pointer; pa[i] is equivalent to *(pa+i). In essence, an expression expressed as a pointer and offset is equivalent to one written as an array and index.

A pointer and an array name differ in one important way that must be remembered. Pa=a and pa++ are acceptable since a pointer is a type of variable. However, an array name is not a variable, hence it is forbidden to use expressions like a=pa and a++.

The location of the first element is supplied when an array name is passed to a function. This argument is a local variable inside the called function, making an array name parameter a pointer—a variable with an address. This information allows us to create a different iteration of the string length calculator, strlen.

```c
int strlen(char *s)
{
int n;
for (n = 0; *s != '\0', s++)
n++;
return n;
}
```

Since s is a pointer, increasing it is totally acceptable; s++ simply increases strlen's private copy of the pointer and has no impact on the character string in the function that called strlen. Thus, strlen("hello, world"), strlen(array), and strlen(ptr) all function as expected.

Both char s[]; and char *s; are equivalent as formal parameters in a function specification, but we prefer the latter since it makes the variable's status as a pointer more clear. When a function receives the name of an array, the function may, at its discretion, interpret the name as either an array or a pointer and act accordingly. In cases where it seems suitable and straightforward, it may even employ both notations.

A pointer to the start of the subarray can be used to pass a portion of an array to a function. For instance, if an is an array, f(&a[2]) and f(a+2) both send the address of the subarray that begins at a[2] to the function f. The argument declaration within f can be written as f(intarr[]) ... or f(int *arr) ... Therefore, it makes no difference to f that the parameter relates to a subset of a bigger array.

It is also feasible to index backwards in an array if one is certain that the items exist; p[-1], p[-2], and so on are syntactically acceptable and refer to the elements that come just after p[0]. Of course, referring to items outside of the array bound is prohibited.

CHAPTER 15 Address Arithmetic

Address Arithmetic:

If p points to an element in an array, p++ advances it to point to the next element, and p+=i advances it to point elements further than it does now. The simplest types of pointer or address arithmetic are those that use this and comparable constructs. With pointers, not all arithmetic operations are possible. The legitimate activities that pointers are capable of doing are

(i) Addition of an integer to a pointer and increment operation.

(ii) Subtraction of an integer from a ponter and decrement operation.

(iii) Subtraction of a pointer from another pointer of same type.

The following arithmetic operations cannot be carried out on pointers:

(i) Addition, multiplication and division of two pointers.

(ii) Multiplication between pointer and any number.

(iii)Division of a pointer by any number.

(iv) Addition of float or double values to pointers.

The correct machine address for the subsequent variable of that type is produced by the equation p+1. other acceptable pointer expressions

p+i, ++p, p+=I, p-q

where the number of array entries between p and q is represented by p-q.

A pointer can be added to in order to traverse an array because it is simply a mem address. P+1 gives a pointer to the following array element.

The * operator has the same amount of precedence as the increment/decrement operators, and they are associative from right to left. In actuality, p+1 increases the memory address by the size of the array element, not by 1.

Assume that x is an integer variable and that p is an integer pointer. The primary challenge now is to determine how the following pointer expressions shown below are to be understood.

(i) x = *p++ is same as two expressions x = *p followed by p = p + 1.

(ii) x = (*p)++ is same as two expressions x = *p followed by *p = *p + 1.

(iii) x=*++p is same as two expressions p=p+1 followed by x=*p.

(iv) x=++*p is same as two expressions *p=*p+1 followed by x=*p

One of the benefits of the language is how pointers, arrays, and address arithmetic are integrated. C is consistent and regular in its approach to address arithmetic. Let's use the creation of a simple storage allocator as an example. Two routines exist. The first, alloc(n), provides the caller with a pointer to n consecutive character locations that can be used to store characters. The second, afree(p), releases the storage that was so gained so that it may be utilised again in the future. The "rudimentary" nature of the routines is due to the requirement that the calls to afree be made in the reverse order of the calls to alloc. In other words, the storage that allocand afree manages is a stack, or last-in, first-out storage. Similar functions called malloc and free from the standard library are available and do not have these limitations.

The simplest method is to allochand out portions of an enormous character array, which we shall refer to as allocbuf. This array has been set aside for exclusive use. No other function needs to know the name of the array because it can be declared static in the source file containing allocand afree and hence be invisible outside of it because they deal in pointers rather than array indices. The array might not even have a name in practical implementations; instead, it might be obtained by executing mallocor and asking the operating system for a pointer to an unnamed storage block. How much of the allocbuf has been used is the other piece of information required. We employ a pointer called allocp that directs attention to the following free element. When allocis requests n characters, it determines whether there is still space in allocbuf. In this case, allocre increments the value of allocp by n to point to the following free area after returning the current value of allocp (i.e., the start of the free block). In the absence of space, allocre yields 0. If p is present in allocbuf, afree(p) essentially sets allocpto p.

```
#define ALLOCSIZE 10000 static char allocbuf[ALLOCSIZE];
static char *allocp = allocbuf; char *alloc(int n)
{
if (allocbuf + ALLOCSIZE - allocp>= n) { allocp += n;
return allocp - n;
} else return 0;
}
void afree(char *p)
{
if (p >= allocbuf&& p <allocbuf + ALLOCSIZE) allocp = p;
}
```

Although often the only relevant values are zero or an expression involving the address of previously declared data of the right type, a pointer can be initialised in general just like any other variable. The character pointer allocp is defined to be a character pointer and initialised to point to the beginning of allocbuf, which is the next free location when the programme starts, by the statement static char *allocp

= allocbuf;. Since the array name is the address of the zeroth element, static char *allocp = &allocbuf[0]; would have been a better alternative. If (allocbuf + ALLOCSIZE - allocp>= n) tests whether there is sufficient space to accommodate a request for n characters. The new value of allocpwould be at most one beyond the end of allocbuf if it were, though it is unlikely. Allocre returns a pointer to the first character in a block of characters if the request can be fulfilled (note the function's declaration). If not, alloc must return some indication that no more space is available. A return value of zero can be used to indicate an unexpected event, in this case no space, because C guarantees that zero is never a suitable address for data.

Integers and pointers cannot be used interchangeably. Zero is the only exception; a pointer may be compared to the constant zero and may have the constant zero allocated to it. As a mnemonic to make it easier to remember that this is a particular value for a pointer, the symbolic constant NULL is sometimes used in place of zero. In'stdio.h', NULL is defined. NULL will be used moving forward. Pointer arithmetic is demonstrated in numerous significant ways by tests like if (allocbuf + ALLOCSIZE - allocp>= n) and if (p >= allocbuf&& p allocbuf + ALLOCSIZE). First, under certain situations, pointers may be compared. Relations like ==,!=,, >=, etc. function correctly if p and q point to elements of the same array. For instance, if p points to an earlier element of the array than does q, then p q is true. Any pointer's equality or inequality with zero can be meaningfully compared. For comparisons or calculations involving pointers that do not point to members of the same array, the behaviour is, nonetheless, undefinable. (There is one exception: pointer arithmetic can utilise the address of the first element past the end of an array.) Second, we've already seen that an integer and a pointer can be added to or removed from each other. The phrase "p + n" refers to the address of the n-th object after the one that "p" is now pointing to. No matter what kind of object p points to, this is true since n is scaled in accordance with the size of the objects p points to, which is defined by the declaration of p. For instance, if an int is four bytes, it will be scaled by four.

Pointer subtraction is also acceptable: q-p+1 is the number of items from p to q inclusive if p and q point to elements of the same array, and p q. This information can be utilised to create still another strlen variant:

```
int strlen(char *s)
{
char *p = s;
while (*p != '\0')
```

```c
p++;

return p - s;

}
```

P is initialised to s, or the first character of the string, in its declaration. Each character is checked individually within the while loop until the final '0' is identified. Since p points to characters, p++ advances p each time to the following character, while p-s provides the number of characters advanced over, or the length of the string. The string might include too many characters to fit in an int. The type ptrdiff_t is large enough to carry the signed difference of two pointer values and is defined in the header file stddef.h>. To match the standard library version, we would use size_t instead of strlen for the return result if we were being cautious. The sizeofoperator's unsigned integer type size_t is what it returns.

Since floats take up more storage space than chars, pointer arithmetic is consistent: if p were a pointer to a float, p++ would move on to the next float. Thus, by just changing char to float throughout allocand afree, we might create a different version of alloc that keeps floats rather than chars. The size of the objects being referred at is automatically taken into account in all pointer manipulations. Assignment of pointers of the same type, addition or subtraction of a pointer and an integer, comparison or subtraction of two pointers to elements of the same array, and assignment or comparison to zero are all acceptable pointer operations. All other pointer maths is forbidden. It is forbidden to assign a pointer of one type to a pointer of another type without a cast, with the exception of void *. It is also forbidden to multiply, divide, shift, mask, add float, or add double to two pointers.

CHAPTER 16 CHARACTER POINTERS AND FUNCTIONS

Character pointers and functions:

The phrase "I am a string" refers to a string constant, which is an array of characters. The array is ended with the null character "0" in the internal representation so that programmes can identify the end. As a result, the length in storage is one character longer than the characters between the double quotes.

String constants are frequently used as function arguments, for example, printf("hello, world");

A character pointer is used to retrieve a character string like this one when it comes in a programme; printf receives a pointer to the array's start. In other words, a pointer to a string constant's initial element is used to access it. Function parameters do not have to include string constants. The sentence pmessage = "now is the time"; assigns a pointer to the character array to pmessage if pmessage is specified as char *pmessage. There are only pointers involved; this is not a string copy. There are no operators in C that can handle a whole string of characters at once. Between these definitions, there is a significant distinction:

char amessage[] = "now is the time";

char *pmessage = "now is the time";

A message is an array that is only large enough to accommodate the character string and '0' used to initialise it. Although the array's individual letters are changeable, a message will always refer to the same storage. Pmessage, on the other hand, is a pointer that is initialised to refer to a constant string. You can change the pointer's location later, but if you try to change the text's contents, the outcome is undefined.

By examining modified versions of two practical functions taken from the standard library, we will show additional features of pointers and arrays. Strcpy(s,t) is the first function, and it copies the string t to the string s. While saying s=t would be good, doing so copies the pointer rather than the characters. We require a loop in order to replicate the characters. First, the array version:

```
void strcpy(char *s, char *t)
{
inti;
i = 0;
while ((s[i] = t[i]) != '\0') i++; }
```

For contrast, here is a version of strcpywith pointers:

```c
void strcpy(char *s, char *t)
{
inti; i = 0;
while ((*s = *t) != '\0')
{ s++; t++; }
}
```

The parameters s and t can be used whenever strcpy sees fit because arguments are supplied by value. Here, they are provided with neatly initialised pointers that are marched down the arrays one character at a time until the '0' that ends t has been copied into s. Strcpy would not be written as we demonstrated above in real life. C programmers with experience would like void strcpy(char *s, char *t)

```c
{
while ((*s++ = *t++) != '\0');
}
```

As a result, the increment of s and t is moved into the loop's test section. The character that t originally pointed to before it was increased is the value of *t++; the postfix ++ doesn't modify t until this character has been fetched. The character is also stored into the former s place before s is increased in the same manner. In order to regulate the loop, this character's value is also compared to "0." Overall, characters up to and including the last "0" are copied from t to s.

The comparison against "0" in the final abbreviation is unnecessary because the only thing being asked is whether the expression is zero. Thus, void strcpy(char *s, char *t) would probably be used to represent the function.

```c
{
while (*s++ = *t++);
}
```

Although this may initially appear confusing, the notational convenience is significant, and the phrase should be grasped since you will regularly encounter it in C programmes. The standard library's (string.h) strcpy function returns the target string as the value of its function. The second procedure we'll look at is strcmp(s,t), which compares the character strings s and t and returns true or false depending on whether s is lexicographically bigger or less than t. The value is calculated by removing the characters where s and t don't agree in the first place.

```c
int strcmp(char *s, char *t)
```

```c
{
inti;
for (i = 0; s[i] == t[i]; i++) if (s[i] == '\0')
return 0;
return s[i] - t[i];
}
```

The pointer version of strcmp:

```c
int strcmp(char *s, char *t)
{
for ( ; *s == *t; s++, t++) if (*s == '\0')
return 0;
return *s - *t;
}
```

There are other, less common pairings of * and ++ and -- because ++ and -- are either prefix or postfix operators. For instance, before obtaining the character that p points to, *--p decreases p. The typical idiom for pushing and popping a stack is really the pair of expressions *p++ = val; val = *--p; The header string.h> provides declarations for the functions covered in this section as well as a number of other string-handling functions from the standard library.

REFERENCES

1. Fundamentals of computer by P K Sinha

2. Programming in C by Reema Thereja

3. Programming in ANSI C by E Balagurusamy

4. O'REILLY, "Practical C Programming", 3rd Edition

5. Yashavant P.kanetkar, "Let Us C", 5th Edition

6. Brian W. kernighan and Dennis M. Ritchie, "The C Programming Language"

7. Greg Perry, "C by Example"

8. Stephen Prata, "C Primer Plus", 5th Edition